SCIENCE PROJECTS

Cells and Systems

Kelly Milner Halls

Heinemann
LIBRARY

www.heinemann.co.uk/library
Visit our website to find out more information about Heinemann Library books.

To order:
- Phone 44 (0) 1865 888066
- Send a fax to 44 (0)1865 314091
- Visit the Heinemann Library Bookshop at www.heinemann.co.uk/library to browse our catalogue and order online.

First published in Great Britain by Heinemann Library, Halley Court, Jordan Hill, Oxford OX2 8EJ, part of Harcourt Education. Heinemann Library is a registered trademark of Harcourt Education Ltd.

Editorial: Joanna Talbot
Design: Kimberly R. Miracle, Fiona MacColl and Ray Hendren
Illustrations: Cavedweller Studios
Picture Research: Melissa Allison
Production: Duncan Gilbert

We would like to thank Nigel Saunders for his assistance in the preparation of this book.

Originated by Dot Gradations Ltd
Printed and bound in China by Leo Paper Group

ISBN 978 0 431 04028 8
11 10 09 08 07
10 9 8 7 6 5 4 3 2 1

British Library Cataloguing in Publication Data
Halls, Kelly Milner, 1957-
Cells and systems. - (Science projects)
1. Cells - Juvenile literature 2. Biological systems - Juvenile literature 3. Cells - Experiments - Juvenile literature 4. Biological systems - Experiments - Juvenile literature
I. Title
571.6

Acknowledgements
The author and publishers are grateful to the following for permission to reproduce copyright material: Alamy, pp. **16** (Phototake Inc), **24** (DK); Corbis/zefa/Thorsten Rother, p. **32**; Getty Images, pp. **8** (Stone), **12**, **40** (3D4Medical.com), **26** (dk), **28** (Photonica); Masterfile/Andrew Douglas, p. **4**; Mediscan/Greenhill, **p. 36**; Science Photo Library, p. **10** (Sinclair Stammers), p. **34** (John Bavosi); Wellcome/Medical Art Service, Munich, p. **20**; Wellcome/Miles Kelly Art Library, p. **6**.

Cover photograph reproduced with permission of Getty Images/Visual Unlimited. Background image by istockphoto.com.

Every effort has been made to contact copyright holders of any material reproduced in this book. Any omissions will be rectified in subsequent printings if notice is given to the publishers.

Contents

» Some words are shown in bold, **like this**. You can find the definitions for these words in the glossary.

Starting your science investigation

A science investigation is an exciting challenge. It starts with an idea that you can test by doing experiments. These are often lots of fun to do. But it is no good just charging in without planning first. A good scientist knows that they must first research their idea thoroughly, work out how they can test it, and plan their experiments carefully. When they have done these things, they can happily carry out their experiments to see if their idea is right.

Your experiments might support your original idea or they might shoot it down in flames. This doesn't matter. The important thing is that you will have found out a bit more about the world around you, and had fun along the way. You will be a happy scientist!

In this book, you'll look at nine science investigations to do with cells and the way our bodies work. You will explore amazing mysteries hidden in the human body.

Do your research

Is there something about your body and how it works that you've always wondered about? Something you don't quite understand but would like to? Then do a little research about the subject. Go to the library and find some books about the subject. Books written for students are often a very good place to start.

Use your favourite Internet search engine to find reliable online resources. Websites written by museums, universities, newspapers and scientific journals are among the best sources for accurate research. Each investigation in this book has some suggestions for further research.

You need to make sure that your resources are reliable when doing research. Ask yourself the following questions, especially about the resources you find online.

The investigations

The start of each investigation contains a box like this.

Possible question

This question is a suggested starting point for your investigation. You will need to adapt the question to suit the things that interest you.

Possible hypothesis

This is only a suggestion. Don't worry if your hypothesis doesn't match the one listed here. Use your imagination!

Approximate cost of materials

Discuss this with your parents before starting work. Don't spend too much.

Materials needed

Make sure you can easily get all of the materials listed and gather them together before starting work.

Level of difficulty

There are three levels of investigations in this book: Easy, Intermediate, and Advanced. The level of difficulty is based on how long the investigation takes and how complicated it is.

1) How old is the resource? Is the information up to date or is it very old?
2) Who wrote the resource? Is the author identified so you know who they are, and what qualifies them to write about the topic?
3) What is the purpose of the resource? A website from a business or pressure group might not give balanced information, but one from a university probably will.
4) Is the information well documented? Can you tell where the author got their information from so you can check how accurate it is?

Some websites allow you to "chat" online with experts. Make sure you discuss this with a parent or teacher first. Never give out personal information online. The "Think U Know" website at http://www.thinkuknow.co.uk has loads of tips about safety online.

Once you know a little more about the subject you want to investigate, you'll be ready to work out your scientific question. You will be able to use this to make a sensible **hypothesis**. A hypothesis is an idea about why something happens that can be tested by doing experiments. Finally, you'll be ready to begin your science investigation!

What is an experiment?

Often when someone says that they are going to do an experiment, they mean they are just going to fiddle with something to see what happens. But scientists mean something else. They mean that they are going to control the **variables** involved in a careful way. A variable is something that changes or can be changed. **Independent variables** are things that you deliberately keep the same or change in your experiment. You should always aim to keep all the independent variables constant, except for the one you are investigating. The **dependent variable** is the change that happens because of the one independent variable that you do change. You make a **fair test** if you set up your experiment so that you only change one independent variable at a time. Your results are **valid** if you have carried out a fair test, and recorded your results or observations honestly.

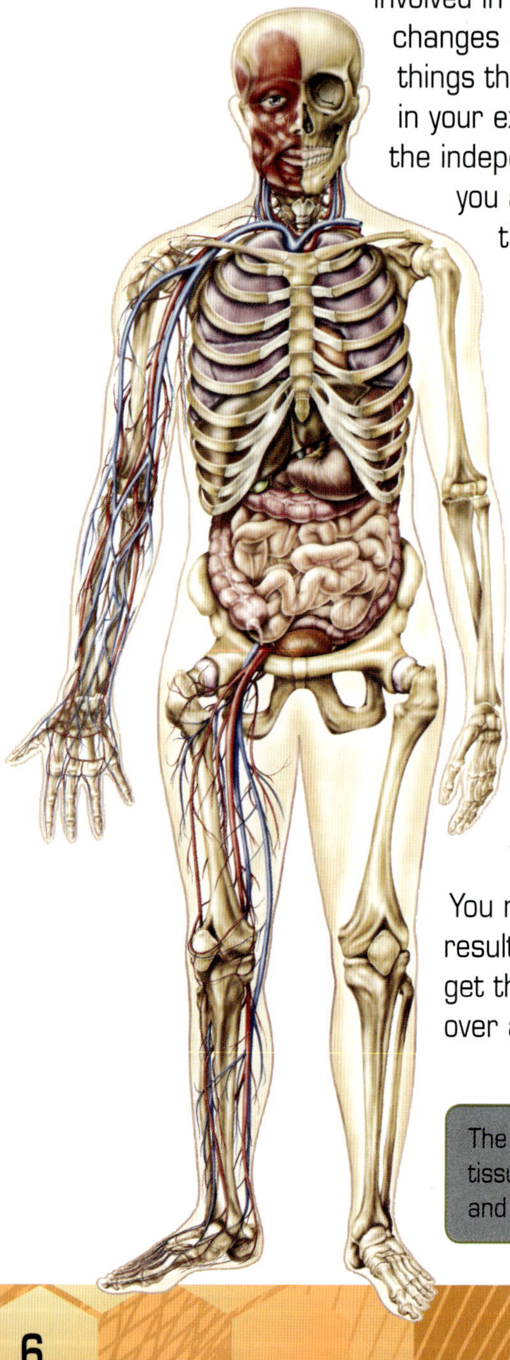

Sometimes you might want to compare one group with another to see what happens. For example, 10 people have headaches. You might give five of them aspirins (Group A) but nothing to the other five (Group B). Group A is your test group, group B your **control** group. The aspirin is the independent variable and the difference in effect on the people in the two groups is your dependent variable.

You must do experiments carefully so that your results are **accurate** and **reliable**. Ideally, you would get the same results if you did your investigation all over again.

The human body contains many tissues and organs, supported and protected by the skeleton

Your hypothesis

Once you've decided on the question you're going to try to answer, you then make a scientific **prediction** of what you'll find out in your science project.

For example, if you're interested in speed, your question might be "Which goes faster when it is pushed, a skateboard or a scooter?" Remember, a hypothesis is an idea about why something happens, which can be tested by doing experiments. So your hypothesis in response to the above question might be, "A skateboard will go faster because it is lighter, and lighter objects go faster when pushed." With a hypothesis, you can also work out if you can actually do the experiments needed to answer your question. Think of a question like: "Can everyone be taught to float in water?" It would be impossible to support your hypothesis, no matter what you make it. This is because you can't possibly test everybody in the world. So, be sure you can actually get the **evidence** needed to support or disprove your hypothesis.

Keeping records

Good scientists keep careful notes in their lab book about everything they do. This is really important. Other scientists may want to try out the experiments to see if they get the same results. So the records in your lab book need to be clear and easy to follow. What sort of things should you write down?

It is a good idea to write some notes about the research you found in books and on websites. You should also include the names of the books or the web addresses. This will save you from having to find these useful resources all over again later. You should also write down your hypothesis and your reasons for it. All your **data** and results should go into your lab book, too.

Your results are the evidence that you use to make your conclusion. Never rub out an odd-looking result or tweak it to "look right". An odd result may turn out to be important later. So you should write down *every* result you get. Tables are a really good way to record lots of results clearly. Make sure you record when you did your experiments, and anything you might have changed along the way to improve them. No detail is too small when it comes to scientific research.

There are tips for making a great report with each investigation and at the end of this book. Use them as guides and don't be afraid to be creative. Make it *your* investigation!

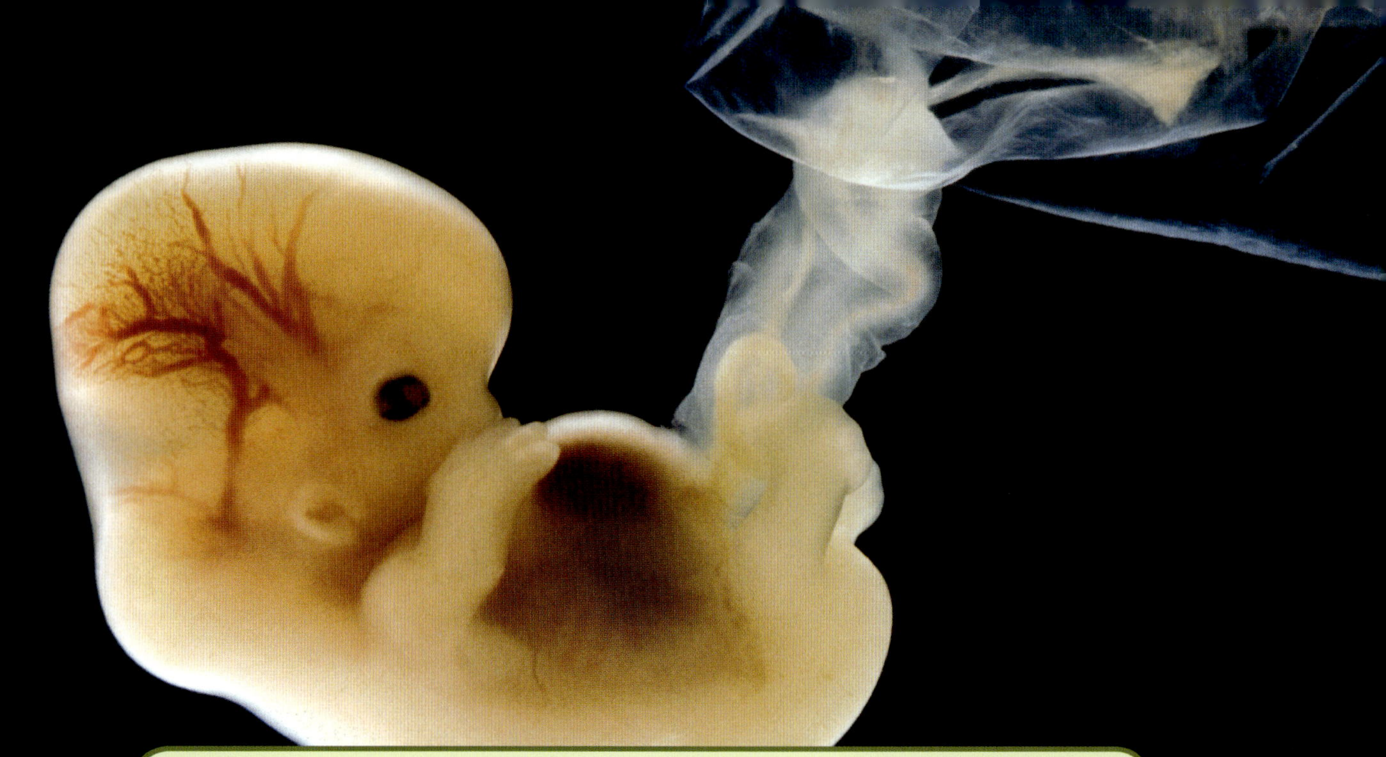

Grow baby grow

A baby spends about 40 weeks in its mother before being born. What is it doing during all that time? How does it change from just one cell to a bouncing baby made of billions of different cells? This investigation will explore these questions by looking at the developmental stages of humans.

Do your research

This investigation looks at the earliest stages of development of humans. It will help to know that the words "fetus", "foetus", and "embryo" are used by doctors and scientists. Before you start your investigation, do some research to find out more about the stages of human development. Once you've done this, you can tackle this investigation. Or, you might come up with an idea of your own after you've learned more about the topic.

You could start your research with this book and these websites:

- *Reproduction*, Steve Parker (Hodder Wayland, 2007)
- Foetal development: http://www.on101.co.uk/foetal.html
- The visible embryo: http://www.visembryo.com

Background information

Possible question

Do humans look the same at all stages of development in the womb?

Possible hypothesis

Yes, they just get bigger.

Level of difficulty

Easy

Approximate cost of materials

£2.00

Materials needed

- Paper
- Glue
- Scissors
- Pens and pencils

Outline of methods

NOTE: This is a research project only, you will not be carrying out an experiment.

1. Research the growth of human embryos from conception (the moment the sperm joins with the egg) to birth (when the baby is born). Include these in your report.
2. Chart the stages of a human embryo on graph paper or using a computer programme. For example, you might plot the length against the time from conception.

Continued

Step 2

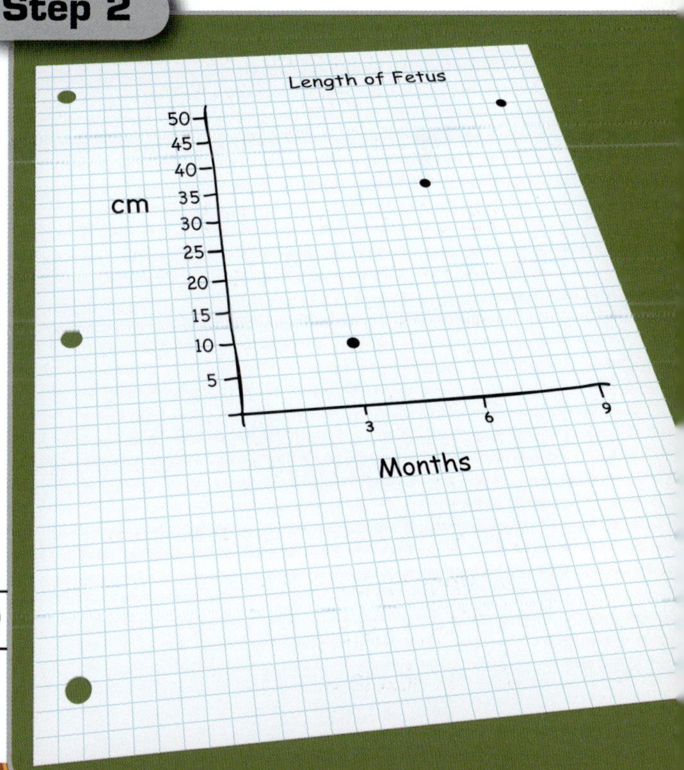

3. Make a timeline to show the main changes at each stage. It would be good to include diagrams or pictures of the embryo in your timeline.

4. Answer these key developmental questions about human embryos:

   When can you see the heart beat?

   When do the eyes form?

   When does movement start?

   When can the embryo hear inside the **womb**?

5. Include any other information about the developing embryo that seems amazing. For example, does the developing embryo ever suck its thumb in the womb?

These are mouse embryos. How do they compare to human embryos?

Analysis of results

- When does the embryo grow the fastest?
- Which resource was the most helpful to you?

More activities to extend your investigation

- Interview your mother, or someone you know well, about what it is like to be pregnant. When could they first feel the baby move? Is that when the baby starts to move or later than that? If there is a difference, why is there one?
- Compare the human embryo to the embryos of different mammals. For example, choose a smaller mammal such as a mouse, and a larger mammal such as a cow or elephant. What are the similarities and differences between them?
- Compare the human embryo to the embryo of a non-mammal, such as a bird, reptile or fish. What are the similarities and differences between them?
- Find out which animals take the longest to develop, and which take the least time. What are the reasons for any differences?
- Compare the growth rates of various animals once they have been born. Why do different animals develop at different rates? How does this help or hinder them?

Project extras

- Make a computer slide show of embryos at different stages of development.
- Collect pictures of embryos of different animals. Make a quiz to see if your classmates can guess what they are.

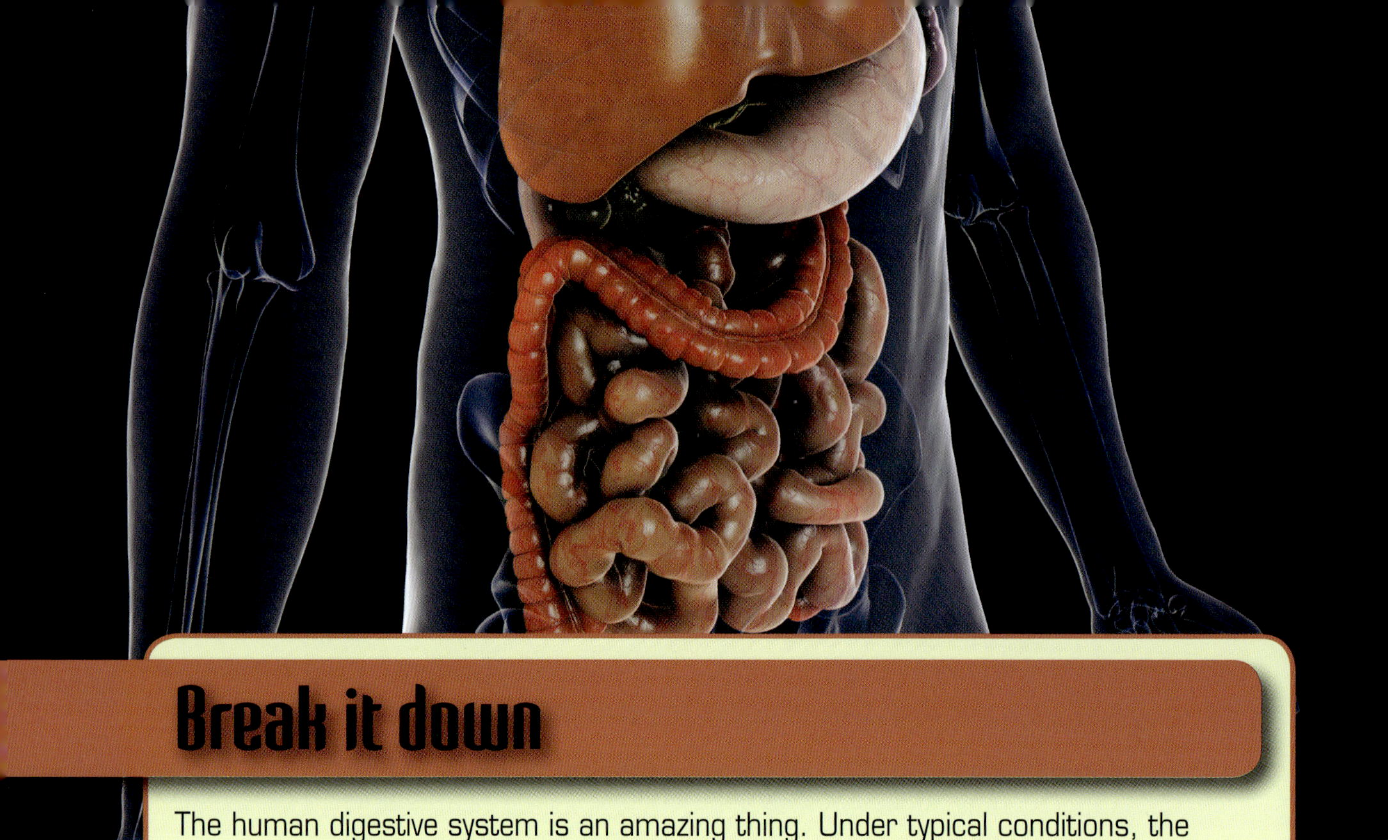

Break it down

The human digestive system is an amazing thing. Under typical conditions, the stomach produces just enough **acid** to break down our food without breaking down our internal organs. But what does this process look like, and how long does it take for different foods to break down in the stomach? This investigation uses vinegar as pretend stomach acid to help you find out.

Do your research

This investigation looks at how food is broken down in the stomach, and how long that process takes for different kinds of food. Before you start your investigation, do some research to find out more about the human stomach and digestive system, and how diet might affect health. Once you've done this, you can tackle this investigation. Or, you might come up with one of your own after you've learned more about the topic.

You could start your research with this book and these websites:

» *Break It Down!*, Steve Parker (Raintree, 2004)

» BBC Health – Healthy living – The digestive system:
http://www.bbc.co.uk/health/healthy_living/nutrition/basics_digestive.shtml

» Discovery kids: http://yucky.kids.discovery.com
(choose "Flash" if you want extra yucky and go to the *Gross and Cool Body* section)

Background information

Possible question

What types of foods are digested more quickly or slowly than others?

Possible hypothesis

Vegetables and fruits are digested more quickly than meat, cheese, and bread.

Level of difficulty

Intermediate

Approximate cost of materials

£5.00

Materials needed

- Two small pieces of bread
- Two small pieces of cooked meat
- Two small pieces of cheese
- Two small pieces of apple
- Two small pieces of lettuce
- 10 small plastic containers
- Lids or cling film as covers
- Permanent marker pen
- Small measuring jug
- 1 litre of distilled white vinegar (ordinary malt vinegar is brown, this is colourless)

Outline of methods

1. Pour 200 ml of vinegar into five of the plastic containers. Mark them with a "V" so you'll remember later which ones contain vinegar.
2. Pour 200 ml of water into the other five plastic containers.
3. Put one piece of each of the five foods into the containers of vinegar.
4. Put the other pieces of the five foods, one each, in the containers of water.

Step 1

Continued

Step 5

5. Cover the containers with lids or cling film to keep the liquids (vinegar or water) in the containers.

6. Check the food pieces every hour for six hours. Record your observations in your lab book.

7. Pay special attention to which foods broke down more easily than others, and whether or not acid or water made any difference.

NOTE: Take care when you remove the lids from the containers of vinegar. Avoid getting too close because the vinegar fumes can be unpleasant and harmful. Make sure you discuss the proper disposal of the food with a responsible adult.

Analysis of results

- Which foods seem to break down the quickest in the acid (vinegar)?
- Which foods did not break down easily in the vinegar?
- Did the vinegar, or the water, make foods break down more quickly?
- How similar is vinegar to stomach acid? What are the differences?

More activities to extend your investigation

- Repeat the experiment but this time use highly processed "junk food", such as a chocolate bar or a bag of crisps.
- Test the acid (vinegar) on other objects, such as chewing gum, coins, plastic, and paper. Make sure you check the ingredients of chewing gum to help you predict what might happen to it. Record your results in your lab book.
- Keep the foods in the containers until they are thoroughly broken down. Check with your parents that this is OK because it may take several days. Check each container twice a day. Record how many days it takes for each food to break down completely.
- Choose the food that breaks down fastest in vinegar. Repeat the experiment with that food. But this time, keep one container of vinegar and food in the fridge, and another container of vinegar and the same food outside the fridge. Is there a difference if the temperature is lower?

Project extras

- Take photos of your foods every hour to show the process in action. Stick the photos in your report.

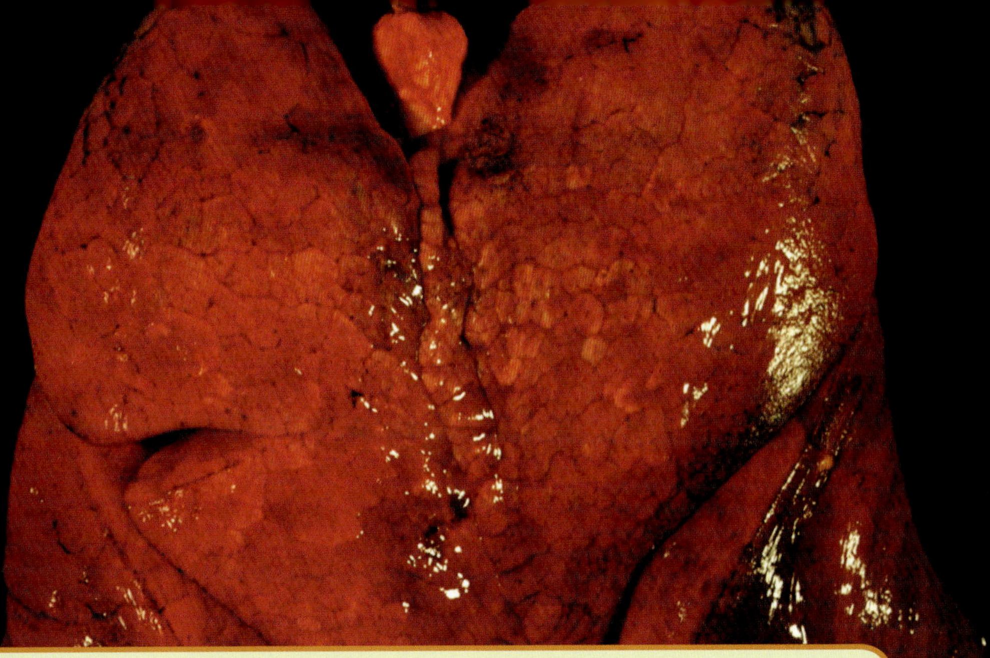

Clearing the air

You know that smoking is bad for your health and can even kill you. If you've ever been curious about what smoke does to your lungs, this investigation will show you what smoke leaves behind.

Do your research

This investigation will show the effects that smoke has on absorbent objects, like your lungs. Before you start your investigation, do some research to find out more about the effects of inhaling various kinds of smoke, the chemicals common in cigarettes, and the medical evidence of the damage smoke can do to the human body. Once you've done this, you can tackle this investigation. Or, you might come up with an idea of your own after you've learned more about the topic.

You could start your research with this book and these websites:

- *Smoking: What's the Deal?*, Jane Bingham (Heinemann Library, 2006)
- Action on Smoking and Health:
  http://www.ash.org.uk
- LifeBytes:
  http://www.lifebytes.gov.uk (then click on "Smoking")
- British Heart Foundation – Why stop:
  http://www.bhf.org.uk/smoking/why.asp

Background information

Possible question

Can we see what smoke leaves behind in the air?

Possible hypothesis

Smoke leaves substances behind that we can see.

Level of difficulty

Intermediate

Approximate cost of materials

£2.50

Materials needed

- One 10 cm by 10 cm square of white, flame-resistant material
- A candle
- Matches
- A long, straight piece of sturdy wire or a wire coat hanger
- Two clothes pegs or two large bulldog clips
- An oven glove
- A piece of cardboard (to display the cloth at the end)
- An adult to supervise

Outline of methods

1. If you do not have a piece of straight wire, take a wire coat hanger. Carefully unwind it, then straighten it out.
2. Fold your piece of cloth in half. Hang it from the wire using a clothes peg or bulldog clip at each unfolded corner.

Step 2

Continued

3. Light the candle. **Ask an adult to help you do this and also Step 4.**

ADULT SUPERVISION NEEDED

4. Put on the oven gloves. Hold the wire so that the fold of the cloth is about 15 cm (6 inches) above the flame. Make sure that the smoke flows up so it touches the fold in the cloth. **Do not hold the cloth too close to the flame**.
5. After five minutes, take the cloth away from the flame and let the wire cool down.
6. Once the wire is completely cold, remove the cloth. Unfold it. Staple it flat, fold side up, to a piece of cardboard. This will preserve the results. Record your observations in your lab book.

Step 4

Step 6

Analysis of results

- How dirty did the smoke make your cloth sample?
- Did both sides of the cloth become dirty, or just the one facing the flame? Why did this happen?
- What do the results tell you about smoking?

More activities to extend your investigation

- Repeat the experiment using a thin slice of raw meat instead of cloth. Raw meat is more similar to our lungs than cloth. Make sure you wear a pair of disposable plastic gloves when working with raw meat.
- Lung tissue is spongy. Repeat the experiment with a piece of bread, which is also spongy.
- Find out which substances in tobacco smoke are responsible for the damage to smokers' health. What is the white material at the end of cigarette meant to do? Does it work?
- Find out about The Great Smog that affected London in 1952. What is smog? How is it made? Why did it kill so many people?

Project extras

- Include in your report photographs of a smoker's lung and a non-smoker's lung. Point out the differences.
- Take photos of your experiments and include them in your report.

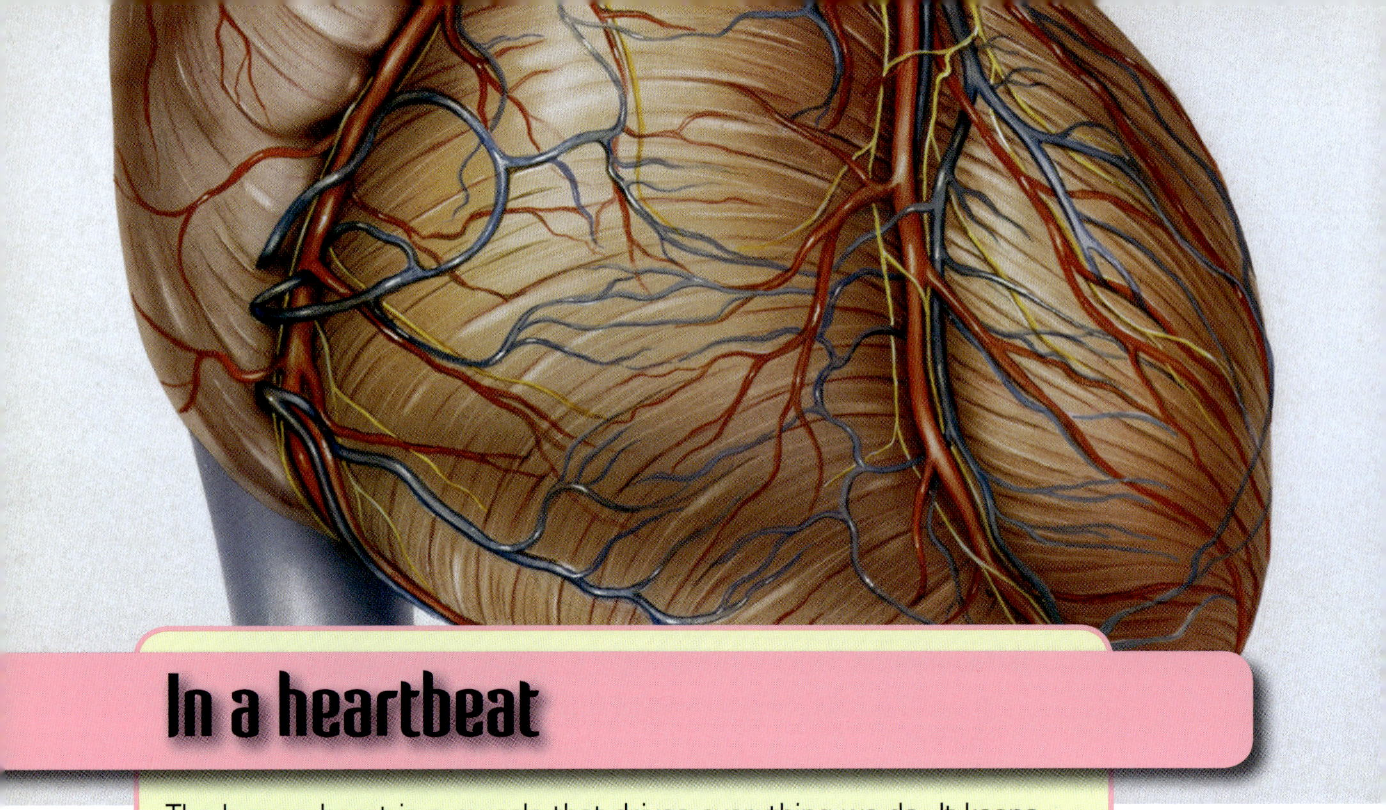

In a heartbeat

The human heart is a muscle that drives everything we do. It keeps beating, whether we are asleep or running around. The heart rate changes depending on whether we're sitting still or we're active. But is it the same for boys and girls? This investigation will help you find out.

Do your research

This investigation looks at the human heart and the effects that rest, activity, and gender have on the heart rate. Before you start your investigation, do some research to find out more about the human heart and the jobs it does in the human body. Find out about the **resting heart rate** and **active heart rate**. You should also find out how to take a pulse accurately. Once you've done this, you can tackle this investigation. Or, you might come up with an idea of your own after you've learned more about the topic.

You could start your research with this book and these websites:

» *Body Systems: Heart and Blood*, Carol Ballard (Heinemann Library, 2003)

» Hyper heart animation:
http://library.med.utah.edu/kw/pharm

» The heart: an online exploration:
http://sln.fi.edu/biosci

Background information

Possible question

Does gender affect the mean resting and active heart rate?

Possible hypothesis

Girls will have a lower mean resting and active heart rate than boys.

Level of difficulty

Intermediate

Approximate cost of materials

Free

Materials needed

- Three boys of similar age, weight and height
- Three girls of similar age, weight and height

  Make sure all of your volunteers feel comfortable exercising. Make sure you ask the volunteers if they have any health conditions that could make this a problem.
- Stopwatch

Outline of methods

1. Ask your volunteers to sit quietly for at least 30 minutes. They could read a book or a magazine during this time.
2. After your volunteers have rested for 30 minutes, check their heart rates one at a time. Feel their **pulse** and see how many beats you can count in 30 seconds. Record this number in your lab book. Also record the gender of your volunteer (girl or boy). Make sure your volunteers are quiet and resting while you do this.
3. Ask one of your volunteers to do 20 star jumps at a quick pace. It shouldn't take more than 40 seconds for the volunteer to do them.
4. Immediately after the last star jump, take the volunteer's heart rate again. Record the number of pulses you can count in 30 seconds, and the gender of your volunteer.
5. Repeat steps 3 and 4 with each volunteer until they have all completed the task, and you have recorded all the results.

Continued

6. Find each volunteer's heart rate in beats per minute. To do this, multiply the number of pulses in 30 seconds by 2.
7. Find the mean resting heart rate in beats per minute for the girls. To do this, add together their heart rates (before the star jumps) and divide this number by three. Do the same thing with their active heart rates (after the star jumps) to find that mean.
8. Follow the same process detailed in step 7 to find the mean resting and active heart rates in beats per minute for the boys.
9. Draw a bar chart to compare the resting heart rates and active heart rates for the girls and the boys.

Step 2

Analysis of results

- Who had the slowest mean resting heart rate, the girls or the boys? Was there a big difference between them?
- Who had the slowest mean active heart rate, the girls or the boys? Was there a big difference between them?
- Whose mean heart rate increased the most after the exercise, the girls or the boys? Was it a big difference?

More activities to extend your investigation

- Try a different exercise with your volunteers to see if you come up with the same results. For example, you could ask them to run for 100 metres, or climb up and down a staircase.
- Compare the boys' and girls' heart rates after researching their lifestyles. For example, what hobbies do they have? Do they play a lot of sport? Could these things affect their heart rates?
- See if your results change when you use older volunteers, such as parents or teachers.
- Try using a larger sample to see if you come up with the same results. For example, you could use 10 boys and 10 girls.

Project extras

- Buy a model of a heart from a toy shop or model shop, and put it together.
- Research the resting heart rates and active heart rates of some famous sports people. Compare these with the results from your investigation.

Eating chocolate for science

Caffeine is a substance found naturally in coffee and chocolate. It is also added to cola drinks, and to some medicines, such as cold and flu remedies. Caffeine is a **stimulant**. This means it can stimulate, or speed up, the body's functions. This investigation looks at how caffeine affects your **resting heart rate**.

Do your research

This investigation looks at the effects caffeine has on a person's resting heart rate. Before you start your investigation, do some research to find out more about the heart and nervous system, and how the intake of caffeine affects them. Once you've done this, you can tackle this investigation. Or, you might come up with an idea of your own after you've learned more about caffeine.

Here are two websites you could start with for your research:

- Growing kids – caffeine and kids
  http://www.growingkids.co.uk/CaffeineAndKids.html
- Neuroscience for kids – caffeine:
  http://faculty.washington.edu/chudler/caff.html

Background information

Possible question

How does caffeine affect a person's resting heart rate?

Possible hypothesis

The more caffeine a person consumes, the faster his or her heart rate will be.

Level of difficulty

Easy

Approximate cost of materials

£6.00

Materials needed

- Five chocolate bars
- Five cans of cola (make sure it is not caffeine-free cola)
- Five volunteers
- A stopwatch

Outline of methods

1. **NOTE:** Before you start your experiment, make sure you ask your volunteers if they are diabetic or have any allergies to the foods you'll be using. Discuss with your parents if your volunteers need to have permission from their parents to take part.
2. Ask the volunteers not to eat or drink anything containing caffeine for 24 hours before your experiment. You will need to give them a list of food and drinks that contain caffeine (you can get this as part of your research).
3. Ask the volunteers if they like cola and chocolate. Record this information for each volunteer in your lab book.
4. Get the volunteers to rest quietly for 15 minutes before you start. They could read a book or magazine during that time.
5. Take the resting heart rate of each of your volunteers. To do this, feel their **pulse** and count the number of beats in 30 seconds. Record this **data** in your lab book.

Continued

6. Now ask all of your volunteers to eat a chocolate bar and drink a full can of cola.
7. Wait 30 minutes. This should be enough time for the effects of the caffeine to start. Now check the resting heart rate of each volunteer again. Record these results in your lab book.
8. For each volunteer's result, multiply the number of pulses in 30 seconds by 2. This gives you their heart rate in beats per minute.

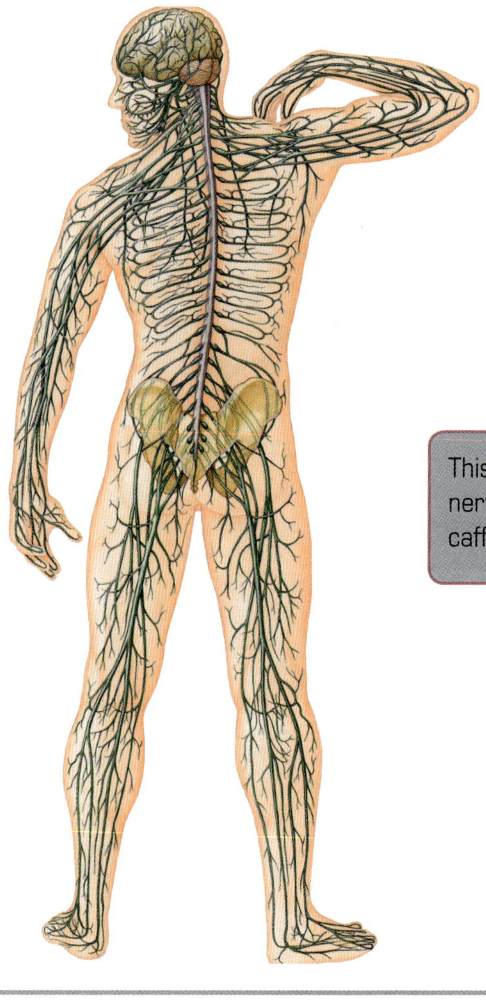

This is a diagram of the nervous system. How does caffeine affect it?

Analysis of results

- Compare each volunteer's resting heart rate, before and after consuming caffeine. Was there a change in their heart rates? Was any change the same for all your volunteers or did some people respond differently?
- Could any observed difference be caused by something else, not just the caffeine? For example, was anybody nervous? Did they have to get up to get their chocolate? Were there any differences between boys and girls?

More activities to extend your investigation

- Repeat the experiment with less caffeine, and see if the resting heart rates change.
- Repeat the experiment but use caffeine-free cola for some volunteers and caffeinated cola for the rest. Do not tell the volunteers that there is no caffeine in some of the colas. Ask an extra person to put the cola drinks into numbered cups for you. Only they should know which contains the caffeinated cola until after the experiment. That way, you won't accidentally influence the results, and any changes should be due only to the caffeine in the drink. This sort of experiment is called a "double-blind trial".
- Increase the time from when your volunteers consume the caffeine and when you take their heart rates. Is there a change?

Project extras

- Use the Internet to research why plants make caffeine and whether caffeine has any effects on other animals. For example, can a spider still make its web properly if it consumes caffeine?

Brain buzz-z-z-z-z

Experts say getting eight to ten hours sleep each night helps your brain and body function properly. But what happens if you stop your body getting the sleep it needs? Is your behaviour or performance altered by lack of sleep? This investigation will answer some of those questions.

Do your research

This investigation looks at how the amount of sleep a person gets affects the way their brain and body works. Before you start your investigation, do some research to find out more about sleep, and what it does for the brain and body. Once you've done this, you can tackle this investigation. Or, you might come up with an idea of your own after you've learned more about sleep and why we need it.

You could start your research with this book and these websites:

- *My Health – Sleep,* Alvin Silverstein and others (Franklin Watts, 2000)
- NINDS (National Institute of Neurological Disorders and Stroke): http://www.ninds.nih.gov/disorders/brain_basics/understanding_sleep.htm
- BBC Science and nature: Human body and mind – sleep: http://www.bbc.co.uk/science/humanbody/sleep/articles/whatissleep.shtml

Background information

Possible question

How does the amount of sleep you get affect brain function and the speed with which you can do simple tasks?

Possible hypothesis

Brain function and physical speed will slow down if you get less sleep.

Level of difficulty

Easy

Approximate cost of materials

Free

Materials needed:

- A partner to help you
- Stopwatch
- Skipping rope
- Tennis ball or similar
- A friend to help you throw and catch the ball
- A page from a book to copy
- Pen
- Paper

Outline of methods

NOTE: Pick a day when you are well rested. You are going to do several tasks. Make sure you do them all on the same day. For each task, ask your partner to time you for exactly one minute. Record the results from each task (steps 1 to 4) in your lab book.

1. Skip as fast as you can for one minute. Count your skips as you go. Record the number of skips in your lab book.
2. See how many times you can catch a ball when another friend throws it easily but quickly from 2 metres away for one minute. Record the number of throws.
3. Copy text from a newspaper article into your lab book. Keep copying for the whole minute and write as fast as you can. Count how many words you were able to copy.
4. See how many words you can come up with in one minute that rhyme with SPOT. Record the number in your lab book.

Continued

5. **NOTE:** Begin the next stage of your investigation on a weekend or other holiday. You are going to have less sleep than usual and it's important that you don't get tired at school. **Check with your parents first**.
6. Go to bed three hours later than you would normally go to bed on a school night. Before you go to sleep, set your alarm clock to wake you up at the time you would normally get up on a school day.
7. Get out of bed when your alarm goes off and, some time today, repeat the same timed tests you did in steps 1 to 4.
8. Plot a scattergram to show your results. Your graph will let you compare how you performed in each task on your well-rested day and on your sleep-deprived day.
9. If you can, repeat the experiment two more times. Make sure you rest for a few days in between each one. Work out the mean of each result.

Step 8

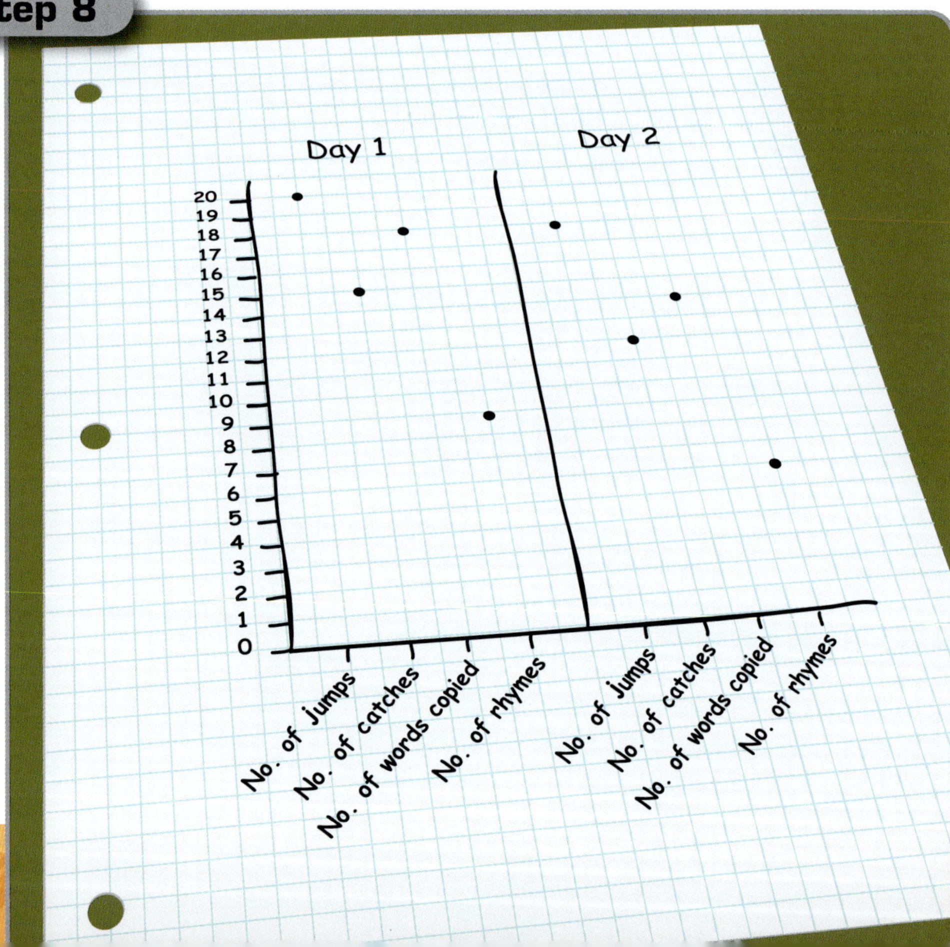

Analysis of results

- Did your scores match? If not, which scores were better?
- Why do you think the results turned out as they did?
- Did the scores change the second and third times you did the experiment? Why or why not?

More activities to extend your investigation

- Record how you felt as you completed the tasks, both on your well-rested day and on your sleep-deprived day. Were there any differences in how you felt?
- Repeat the same tasks on a day when you eat a healthy diet, then on a day when you eat a junk-food diet, but when you have the same amount of sleep. Compare the effects of diet and sleep on your scores.
- Investigate whether drinking a cola drink improves your ability to complete the tasks on your sleep-deprived day.

Project extras

- Use the Internet to find out what rules apply to people who have to work long hours, or who have to work through the night.

Cheesy feet

You may have a favourite team or sports person, but would you want to smell their shoes? Nothing clears a room more quickly than someone taking off a pair of pongy trainers. But what makes them pong? This investigation helps solve the mystery of the stinky shoes.

Do your research

This investigation looks at your outer layer – the skin. It is the largest organ of the human body and it is also called the **epidermis**. In this investigation, you will wrap your foot in a plastic bag. This may affect your circulation, so if you have any medical conditions, make sure you discuss the investigation with a parent or doctor first. Do some research to find out more about skin, its parts, and how they work. Once you've done this, you can tackle this investigation. Or, you might come up with an idea of your own after you've learned more about sweaty feet and smells.

You could start your research with this book and these websites:

- *Smelling and Tasting*, Alvin Silverstein and others (Twenty-First Century Books, 2002)
- The smell report – the human sense of smell: http://www.sirc.org/publik/smell_human.html
- BBC Health – Ask the doctor – sweaty feet: http://www.bbc.co.uk/health/ask_the_doctor/sweatyfeet.shtml

Background information

Possible question

What makes trainers smell bad?

Possible hypothesis

Sweat from the skin's sweat glands makes trainers smell bad.

Level of difficulty

Easy

Approximate cost of materials

£15.00

Materials needed:

- A new, or clean, pair of trainers in your size
- A permanent marker pen
- 16 large plastic bags
- 7 pieces of string
- 5 brave sniffing volunteers

Outline of methods

1. Take the trainers and mark the right shoe with a big X. Leave the other without a mark.
2. Before you begin your daily routine, put your right foot inside two plastic bags, so that your foot is wrapped in a double layer of plastic.
3. Tie a string firmly, but not too tightly, around your ankle to keep the plastic bags from slipping down into your shoe.
4. Put the shoe marked with the X on your bagged foot.
5. Wear the other shoe without a sock or any other barrier between your foot and the lining of the shoe.

Step 3

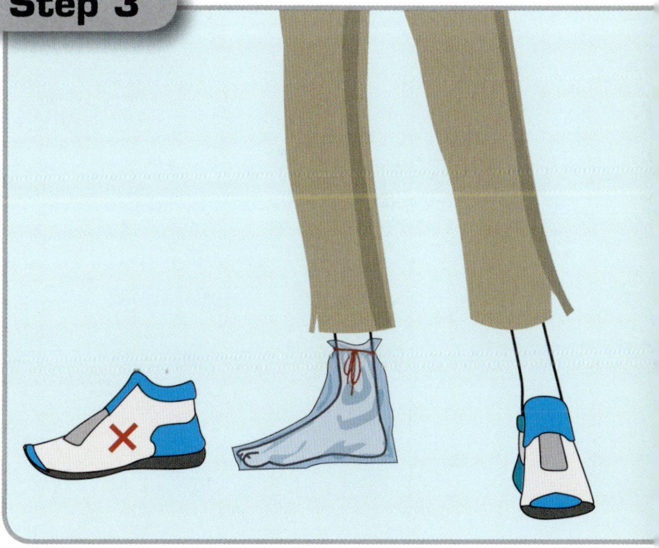

Continued

6. Do 30 star jumps or some other physical activity that makes your body, and especially your feet, sweat.
7. Take off the shoes and bags. The experiment is finished for today.
8. Repeat steps 2 to 7 for a full week.
9. At the end of the week, put each trainer in a separate, new plastic bag. Tie off the tops of the bags. Put both bags in a dark, moist place for another full week. A corner of the bathroom may do here.
10. At the end of the week, ask your sniffing volunteers to decide which shoe smells worse. Record in your lab book which shoes each volunteer felt smelled the worst. Also record how bad they thought each shoe smelled as "really strong", "strong", "mild", or "OK".
11. Make a tally of how many volunteers chose each shoe as the worst.

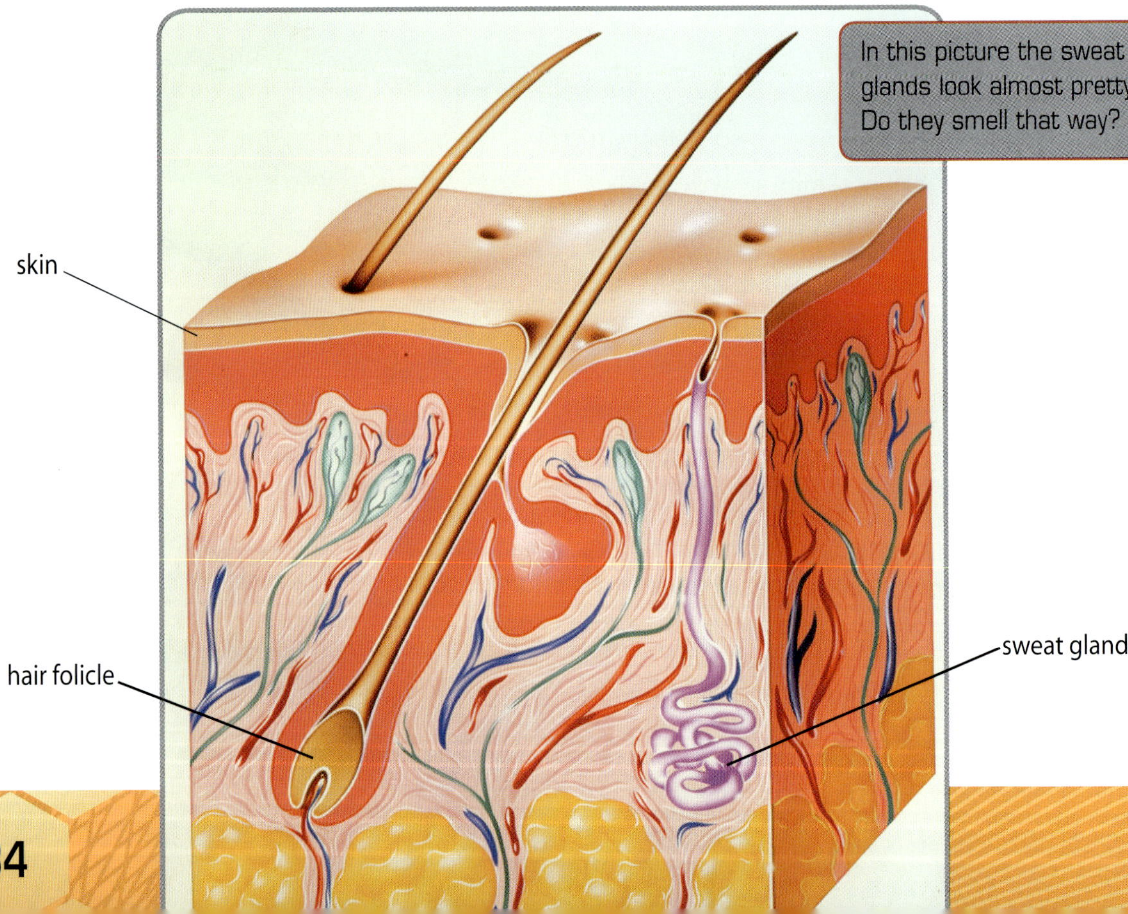

In this picture the sweat glands look almost pretty. Do they smell that way?

Analysis of results

- Which foot sweated the most, the one in plastic or the other foot? Did this sweaty foot feel hotter, colder, or the same as the other foot after doing your exercises?
- Which shoe was judged the worst by the majority of your volunteers? How bad did they think it smelled?
- Did the sweatiest foot produce the smelliest shoe?
- Why did one shoe smell worse than the other?

More activities to extend your investigation

- Repeat the experiment with another new or clean pair of trainers, using a sock in one shoe, and no sock in the other. Compare the results.
- Some socks are sold as being able to neutralise foot odours. Wear an ordinary sock on one foot and one of the special socks on the other foot. Wear your shoes for a day as normal, for example, on a school day. Ask your volunteers to rate each sock for smelliness at the end of the day. Repeat the experiment with new socks, but swap which sock goes on which foot. This will check whether one foot is naturally smellier than the other.

Project extras

- Make a cross-section of the epidermis. You could draw a picture or make a model.
- Use the Internet to find out why the armpits can get smelly.

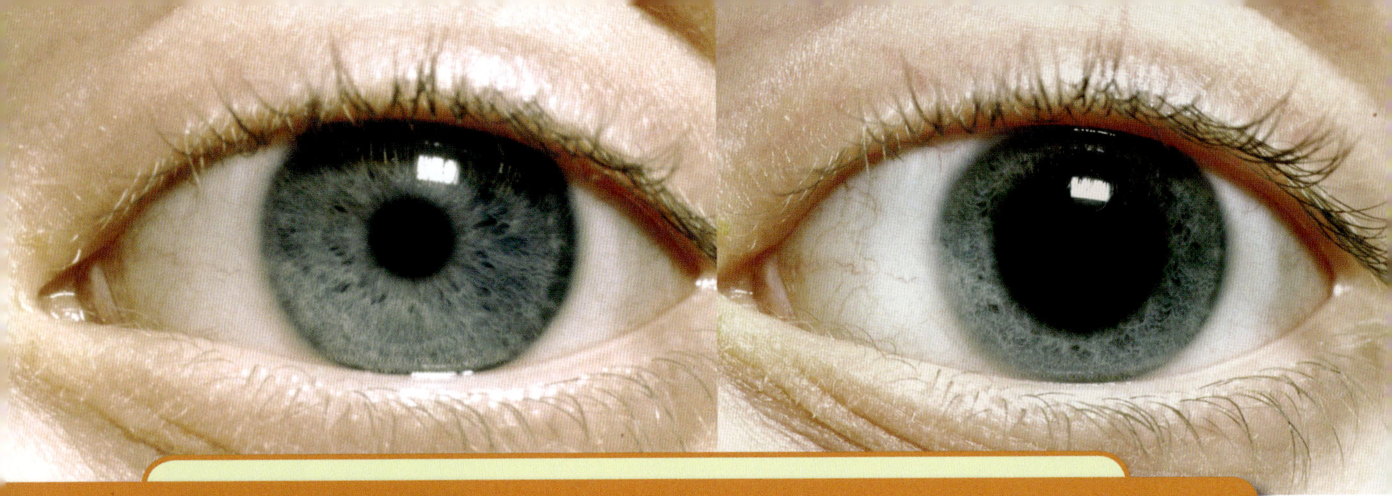

Don't look!

Have you ever noticed that when a light flashes, we stop and take notice? Perhaps that's why there are so many flashing signs in towns and cities – so that shops and advertisers can get our attention. But is this an **involuntary** response? What about different coloured lights? Do we respond involuntarily to these too? This investigation will explore how the eye reacts to different kinds of light.

Do your research

This investigation looks at the human eye and its reaction to light. Before you begin your project, do some research to find out more about the human eye, how it works, and reflex actions. Once you've done this, you can tackle this investigation. Or, you might come up with an idea of your own after you've learned more about the human eye.

You could start your research with this book and these websites:

- *The Senses*, Steve Parker (Hodder Wayland, 2003)
- A big look at the eye: http://www.kidshealth.org/kid/body/eye_SW.html
- Healthy eyes: http://www.healthyeyes.org.uk

Background information

Possible question

Will the pupils of the human eye react differently to lights of different colour?

Possible hypothesis

Some colours will cause a bigger reaction in the pupils.

Level of difficulty

Easy

Approximate cost of materials

£10.00

Materials needed

- Four small torches (**not laser pens**)
- Transparent coloured plastic sheets in three different colours. These must be big enough to cover the ends of the torches. For small torches, coloured sweet wrappers are a cheap way to get the plastic you need.
- Three rubber bands
- Four volunteers (two boys, two girls)

Outline of methods

1. Make sure you tell your volunteers in advance what you plan to do. It will stop them feeling uneasy as the experiment goes along.
2. Wrap the coloured plastic over the ends of three of the torches. Use the rubber bands to stop the plastic falling off. You should now have three torches that each make a different coloured beam of light, and an ordinary torch.
3. Make sure that the room is dimly lit, but not completely dark!

Step 2

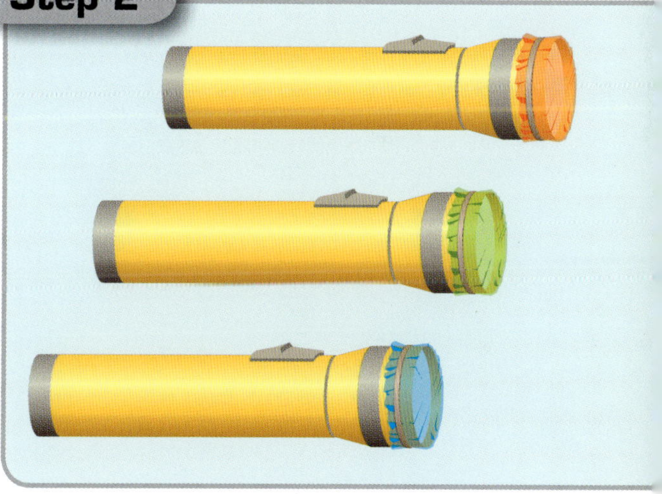

Continued

4. Ask one of your volunteers to come in. Ask him or her to sit down on a chair and relax.

5. While they are relaxing, look at their pupils. Don't use a torch at this stage. How big is the pupil (the black part) compared to the iris (the coloured part)? Do they change in size as your volunteer rests or do they stay the same? Record your results in your lab book. You may want to include a simple drawing to show the size of the pupils.

6. Tell your volunteer that you are starting the next stage of the experiment.

7. Briefly flash one of the four torches in the direction of the volunteer so that they can definitely see it. It could be a simple flash of light, or it could be a light turned on for a few seconds and then turned off. Any significant change in the room's lighting will do, but make sure you do the same thing each time.

8. Observe your volunteer's reaction, including whether or not their pupils change size. Record your observations in your lab book. You may want to include a simple drawing to show the size of the pupils. You could try to measure the diameter of the pupils, but take care not to let the ruler touch the volunteer's eye.

Step 8

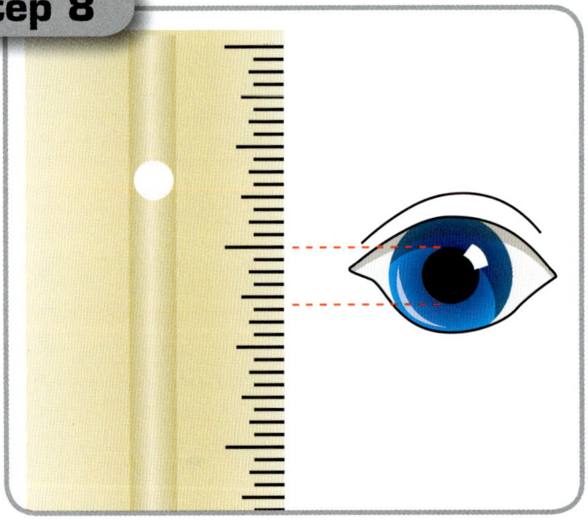

9. Repeat steps 7 and 8 with each torch, making sure you do exactly the same thing each time. Record all your results in your lab book.

10. Repeat steps 3 to 9 with each of your remaining volunteers. Again, make sure you are consistent in how you use the torches with each volunteer.

Analysis of results

- Did the volunteers' pupils stay the same size at the start, or did they change? Did they get bigger or smaller?
- Did the different lights affect the pupils in the same way?
- Did male and female volunteers have the same reactions?

More activities to extend your investigation

- Repeat the experiment in a brightly lit room, rather than a dimly lit room.
- Investigate if wind affects the pupils. *Gently* puff into one eye or use a small fan blowing in the volunteer's face.
- What happens if you cover one eye with a blindfold? Do you get the same results as before?

Project extras

- In ordinary daylight, ask your volunteers to shut their eyes for a few seconds, then open them again. What happens to the size of their pupils? Use the Internet to find out why this happens.

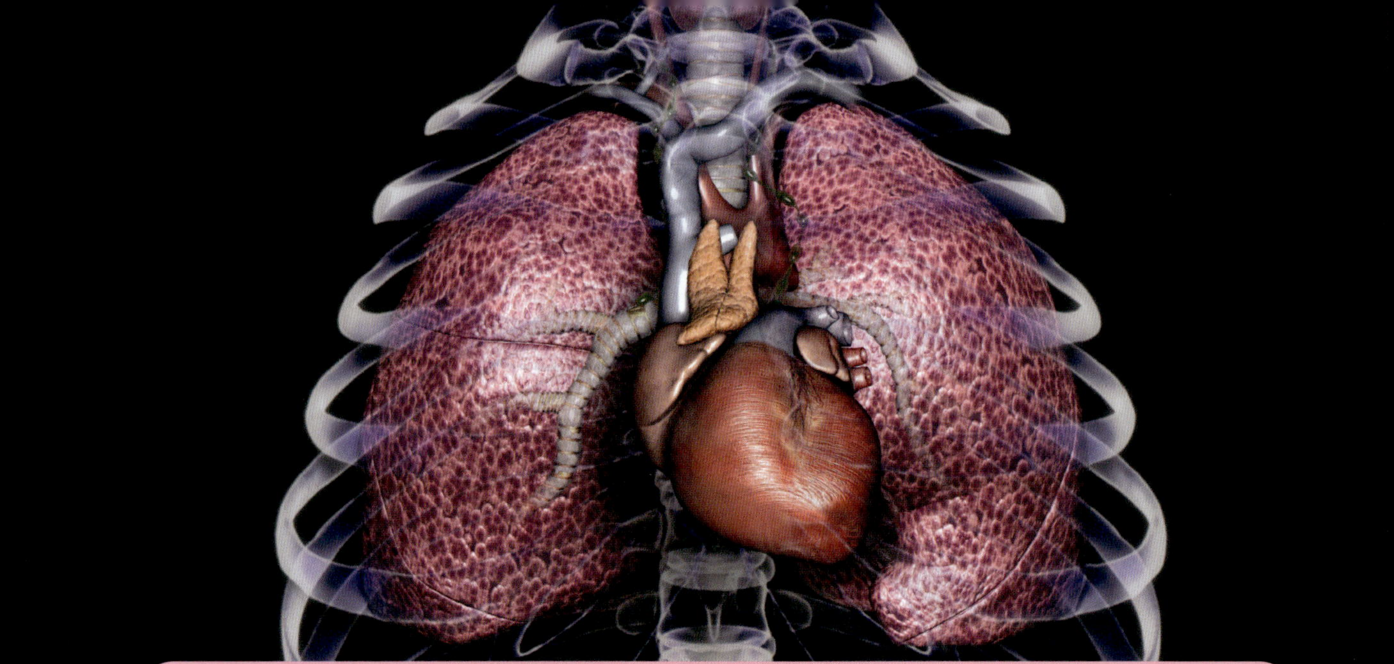

A lungful of air

Our lungs contain about two and a half kilometres of airways and more than 300 million tiny air sacs called alveoli. The lungs are where our bodies absorb oxygen from the air and release waste carbon dioxide. This is called gas exchange. Red blood cells carry oxygen from the lungs to the cells in your body. The watery part of the blood, called the plasma, carries waste carbon dioxide from the cells to the lungs. All this happens without you ever even thinking about it! But have you ever wondered if all lungs are the same size? This investigation will explore that question.

Do your research

This investigation looks at how much air the lungs can hold. The **vital capacity** of the lungs is the amount of air you can breathe out after taking your biggest breath. You will make and use your own measuring device, called a **spirometer**. Before you start your investigation, do some research to find out more about the lungs and how they work. Once you've done this, you can tackle this investigation. Or, you might come up with an idea of your own after you've learned more about the lungs.

You could start your research with this book and website:

» *Heart, Lungs and Blood*, Steve Parker (Hodder Wayland, 2007)

» Your gross and cool body – respiratory system:
http://yucky.kids.discovery.com/flash/body/pg000138.html

Background information

Possible question

Does gender affect a person's vital capacity?

Possible hypothesis

Yes, boys will have a bigger mean vital capacity than girls.

Level of difficulty

Advanced

Approximate cost of materials

£5.00

Materials needed

- 10 volunteers (5 girls and 5 boys)
- One permanent marker pen
- One empty 5 litre mineral water bottle with its cap
- One piece of flexible plastic tubing, 60 cm long
- One measuring jug (a 500 ml jug or a 1 litre jug)
- One large bucket, able to hold at least 5 litres of water. A car wash bucket is ideal, as these are large and wide.

Outline of methods

Make a spirometer:

1. Add half a litre (500 ml) of water to the empty mineral water bottle using the measuring jug. Draw a line with the marker at the top of the water level. Repeat this nine more times. Your bottle will be full of water, and it will have measuring lines on it. Put the cap on it.
2. Add enough water to your bucket so that you can submerge the capped end of the mineral water bottle.
3. Turn your bottle upside down and submerge it in the bucket. **Take care because it will be heavy**. Remove the cap under the water. This will stop any air getting back in.

Continued →

Step 9

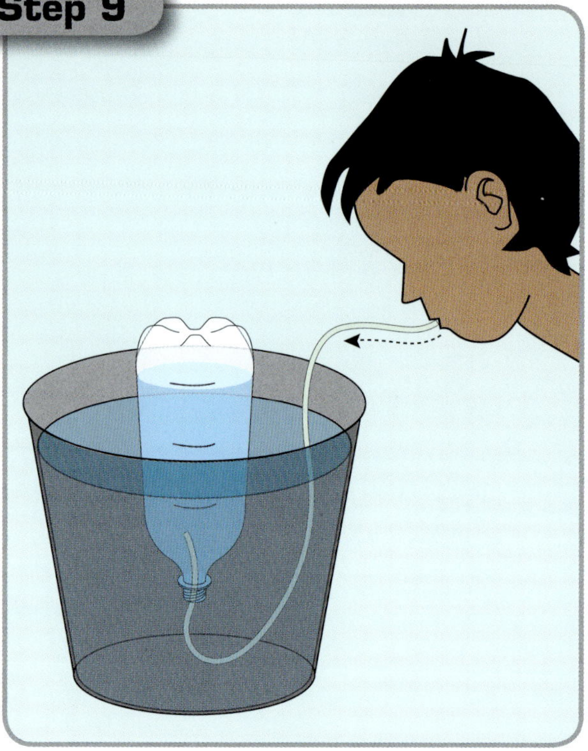

4. Put one end of your plastic tubing into the mineral water bottle in the water. Leave the other end outside the water. This is the tube your volunteers will breathe into, so that you can find out their lung capacity.
5. Make sure you have a place where you can test all 10 of your volunteers in one day. You want to make sure that they are breathing the same air, so that your results will be reliable.
6. Tell your volunteers that you'll be testing their lung capacity, one at a time, and recording the results.
7. Get a volunteer to take a deep breath. They should then breathe out into the tubing for as long as they can without straining themselves too much.
8. Make a good estimate of the amount of air your volunteer exhaled by measuring how much the bottle fills with air. Remember that each line on the bottle represents a half litre, starting from the top down.
9. Write this number down in your lab book. This is the amount of air that your volunteer's lungs can hold (the vital capacity).
10. Take out the plastic tubing and refill the bottle with water.
11. Wash the mouth end of the tubing thoroughly with soap and water or diluted disinfectant and repeat steps 3 to 10 for your next volunteer.
12. Repeat steps 3 to 10 two more times for each volunteer. Record all of the results in your lab book.

13. Work out a mean vital capacity for each of your volunteers. Do this by adding their three results together and dividing by three. Record these mean values in your lab book.

14. Work out a mean vital capacity for the girls. Do this by adding all their results together and dividing by the number of results. Record this mean value in your lab book. Do the same thing for the boys' results.

15. Work out the difference between the girls' mean results and the boys' mean results from step 14.

Analysis of results

- Which gender, girls or boys, had the biggest mean vital capacity? Suggest some reasons for this.
- Were the individual mean vital capacities similar to each other, or did some volunteers have a much smaller or larger vital capacity? Suggest some reasons for this. For example, were all the volunteers similar in height, age and weight?

More activities to extend your investigation

- Test volunteers of different ages and see if your results are the same.
- Test sporty volunteers and non-sporty volunteers to see if that makes a difference in mean vital capacity.
- Test some volunteers indoors and some outdoors to see if the difference in air gives different results.

Project extras

- Take photos of your spirometer and include them in your report.
- Draw a colour diagram of the lungs and respiratory system.

Writing your report

In many ways, writing the report of your investigation is the hardest part. You've researched the science involved, and you've had fun gathering all your evidence together. Now you have to explain what it's all about.

You are the expert

Very few other people, if any, will have done your investigation. So you are the expert here. You need to explain your ideas clearly. Scientists get their most important investigations published in a scientific magazine or journal. They may also stand up at meetings and tell other scientists what they have found. Or they may display a large poster to explain their investigation. You might consider giving a talk or making a poster about your investigation, too. But however scientists present their investigations, they always write it down first – and you must too. Here are some tips about what you should include in your report.

Some hints for collecting your results

- **Making a table:** Tables are great for recording lots of results. Use a pencil and ruler to draw your table lines, or make a table using a word processing program. Put the units (m, s, kg, N and so on) in the headings only. Don't write them into the main body of your table. Try to make your table fit one side of paper. If you need two sheets of paper, make sure you write the column headings on the second sheet as well.
- **Recording your results:** It is often easy to forget to write down your results as they come in. Or you might just scribble them onto the back of your hand – and then wash your hands! A wise scientist will always make a neat, blank table in their lab book before starting. They will write down their results as they go along and not later on.
- **Odd stuff:** If something goes wrong, make a note of it. This will remind you which results might not be reliable.
- **Precision:** Always record your readings to the precision of your measuring equipment. For example, if you have scales that show 24.6 g, don't write 24 or 25 in your table. Instead, write 24.6 because that's the precise measurement.

Laying out your report

You could use the following headings to organise your report in a clear manner:

- **A title**
  This gives an idea of what your investigation is about.
- **Aims**
  Write a brief outline of what you were trying to do. It should include the question you were trying to answer.
- **Hypothesis**
  This is your scientific prediction of what will happen in your investigation. Include notes from your research to explain why you think your prediction will work out. It might help to write it out as: "I think ... will happen because ..."
- **Materials**
  List the equipment you used to carry out your experiments. Also say what any measuring equipment was for. For example, "scales (to weigh the objects)".
- **Methods**
  Explain what you actually did in your investigation.
- **Results**
  Record your results, readings and observations clearly.
- **Conclusions**
  Explain how closely your results fitted your hypothesis. You can find out more about this on the next page.
- **Bibliography**
  List the books, articles, websites or other resources you used in your research.

And finally ... the conclusions

There are two main bits to your conclusions. These are the "Analysis" and the "Evaluation". In the analysis you explain what your evidence shows, and how it supports or disproves your **hypothesis**. In the evaluation, you discuss the quality of your results and their reliability, and how successful your methods were.

Your analysis

You need to study your **evidence** to see if there is a relationship between the **variables** in your investigation. This can be difficult to spot in a table, so it is a good idea to draw a graph. You should always put the **dependent variable** on the vertical axis, and the **independent variable** on the horizontal axis. The type of graph you need to draw depends on the type of variables involved:

- A bar chart if the results are **categoric**, such as hot/cold, male/female.
- A line graph or a scattergram if both variables are **continuous**, such as time, length, or mass.

Remember to label the axes to say what each one shows, and the unit used. For example, "time in s" or "height in cm". Draw a line or curve of best fit if you can.

Explain what your graph shows. Remember that the reader needs help from you to understand your investigation. Even if you have spotted a pattern, don't assume that your reader has. Tell them. For example, "My graph shows that the higher up the ball was dropped, the higher it bounced". Circle any points on your graph that seem **anomalous** (too high or too low).

Your evaluation

Did your investigation go well, or did it go badly? Was your evidence good enough for you to support or disprove your hypothesis? Sometimes it can be difficult for you to answer these questions. But it is really important that you try. Scientists always look back at their investigations. They want to know if they could improve their methods next time. They also want to know if their evidence is **reliable** and **valid**. Reliable evidence can be repeated with pretty much the same results. Valid evidence is reliable, and it should answer the question you asked in the first place. As before, remember that you are the person who knows your investigation the best. Don't be afraid to show off valid evidence. And be honest if it's not!

Glossary

accurate close to the true value

acid a type of chemical that can burn

active heart rate number of times the heart beats per minute when the body is exercising

anomalous a result that seems out of place, such as too high or too low

categoric a variable that can be given labels, such as male/female

continuous a variable that can have any value, such as weight or length

control something that is left unchanged in order to compare results against it

data measurements or observations made in an experiment

dependent variable the variable that changes because of what you do in an experiment

epidermis skin

evidence data that has been checked to see if it is valid

fair test an experiment in which you only change one variable at a time

hypothesis an idea about why something happens that can be tested by experiments

independent variable a variable that you deliberately keep the same or change in an experiment

involuntary not by choice or not controlled by the mind

prediction to say in advance what you think will happen based on a scientific idea

pulse the beat that can be felt on the wrist or neck caused by the heart pumping blood through the arteries.

reliable results that can be repeated

resting heart rate number of times the heart beats per minute when the body is not exercising

spirometer equipment that measures the volume of air entering and leaving the lungs

stimulant substance that increases activity in the mind or body

valid results from a fair test

variable something that changes or can be changed

vital capacity the volume of air that someone can breathe out after taking their biggest breath

womb organ in the female body where the unborn baby grows

Index